21st
Century
Skills Library

P9-CBK-412

COOL MILITARY CAREERS

HELICOPTER CREW CHIEF

WIL MARA

CHERRY
LAKE
Publishing

Published in the United States of America by
Cherry Lake Publishing, Ann Arbor, Michigan
www.cherrylakepublishing.com

Content Adviser
Cynthia Watson, PhD, author of *U.S. National Security*

Credits
Cover and page 1, ©STT0005881/Media Bakery; pages 4, 12, 13, 16, 20, 23, 27, and 29, U.S. Marine Corps photo by Lance Cpl. Robert R. Carrasco/Released; page 6, U.S. Navy photo by Mass Communication Specialist Seaman Betsy Lynn Knapper/Released; page 9, U.S. Marine Corps photo by Lance Cpl. Tammy K. Hineline/Released; page 10, U.S. Marine Corps photo by Cpl. Samantha H. Arrington /Released; page 15, U.S. Marine Corps photo by Cpl. Benjamin R. Reynolds/Released; page 18, U.S. Army photo by Staff Sgt. Garrett Ralston/Released; page 24, U.S. Army photo by Sgt. Sean P. Casey/Released; page 26, U.S. Army photo by Spc. Roland Hale/Released

Copyright ©2013 by Cherry Lake Publishing
All rights reserved. No part of this book may be reproduced or utilized in any form or by any means without written permission from the publisher.

Library of Congress Cataloging-in-Publication Data
Mara, Wil.
    Helicopter crew chief/by Wil Mara.
      p. cm.—(Cool military careers)
    Includes bibliographical references and index.
    Audience: Grades 4–6.
    ISBN 978-1-61080-449-3 (lib. bdg.) — ISBN 978-1-61080-536-0 (e-book) —
ISBN 978-1-61080-623-7 (pbk.)
    1. Helicopters—United States—Juvenile literature. 2. Airmen—United States—
Juvenile literature. 3. United States—Armed Forces—Vocational guidance—Juvenile
literature. I. Title.
    UG1233.M37 2012
    358.4'183—dc23   2012002153

Cherry Lake Publishing would like to acknowledge
the work of The Partnership for 21st Century Skills.
Please visit *www.21stcenturyskills.org* for more information.

Printed in the United States of America
Corporate Graphics Inc.
July 2012
CLFA11

R0442957051

TABLE OF CONTENTS

CHAPTER ONE
A MOST AMAZING MACHINE

Kevin is awoken from a deep sleep by screams of *"The mission is a 'go'! Let's move! LET'S MOVE!"* He leaps out of bed, barely awake, and pulls on his uniform. Minutes

Crew chiefs make sure that helicopters are always ready to fly at a moment's notice.

later, he is running across the **tarmac** with the rest of his crew. Up ahead sits a military helicopter, its **blades** sitting quietly in the morning light. It is a machine like no other, with awesome speed, fierce power, and the most advanced technical equipment in the world. Kevin's job as the helicopter's crew chief is to make sure it runs exactly the way it's supposed to. If there's a problem during the mission, it will be his fault. But if it flies perfectly, he'll look like a hero.

Kevin and his team swarm around the "bird," each person doing a different job. One checks the electronic equipment, another the fluids, and another the weapons. Once Kevin is certain that the vehicle is in perfect running order, he gives the word to the pilot and copilot. They climb in and get it started. The blades begin to spin until they are a whirling blur.

Kevin climbs inside the helicopter and goes to the back, continuing to make sure every piece of equipment is working correctly. The pilot receives the signal to lift off, and the copter begins to climb skyward. Through the window, the world is shrinking. Kevin can tell from the hum of the blades and the groan of the engine that the aircraft is performing beautifully. He feels very proud—but only for a moment. The mission has just begun. There's still plenty of work ahead.

■ ■ ■

A helicopter is different than other types of aircraft. It can take off straight up, land straight down, and fly both forward and backward. It can also **hover**, or stay in the air without moving in any direction. Humans have dreamed about this kind of flight for thousands of years. Leonardo da Vinci, one of the greatest creative minds in history, made sketches of a flying

Unlike other aircraft, helicopters are capable of hovering.

machine somewhat similar to the helicopter. The great American inventor Thomas Edison worked on helicopter designs in the 1880s, although he was never able to build one that worked.

The first helicopters that functioned reliably were developed in the 1930s. During World War II (1939–1945), the U.S. military used helicopters in battle. Since then, military copters have been greatly improved both mechanically and technologically. Today, a military helicopter is such a complex vehicle that it requires a team of highly trained people to keep it in top working order. The crew chief is the person who oversees this team of technicians.

LIFE & CAREER SKILLS

As a helicopter crew chief in the military, you'll learn how to think clearly in order to make critical decisions in difficult situations. You'll also learn how to lead other members of your team. You'll be taught how to be responsible for your own actions and how to focus on a goal until you've achieved it. These skills will contribute not only to your value to the armed forces but also to your personal growth and maturity.

A crew chief's job is to make sure the helicopter to which he or she has been assigned is always ready to go at a moment's notice. The crew chief may be in charge of other people who do the actual hands-on work. These men and women replace worn or broken parts, test communications equipment, and reload weapons. The crew chief is responsible for making sure these tasks are carried out correctly.

A crew chief may also be required to fly on the copter during a mission. Some missions can be simple, such as transporting soldiers or investigating the geography of an area to gain information that has military value. Others can be quite dangerous, such as search and rescue of wounded soldiers or actual combat with enemy forces. In these situations, a crew chief's life may be put in danger. Crew chiefs even have to be prepared to fire weapons when needed.

The helicopter crew chief is among the military's many unsung heroes. These are the people who perform important and often dangerous jobs but are frequently unknown to the rest of the world. Yet you can be sure that every time one of those mighty birds lifts off from the ground and comes back in one piece, a crew chief had something to do with its success.

Helicopters are a fast and effective way to transport soldiers.

CHAPTER TWO

BECOMING A HELICOPTER CREW CHIEF

To become a helicopter crew chief in the military, you first have to join the military. There are five main branches of the

Helicopter crew chiefs play important roles in all five branches of the military.

U.S. military: the Army, the Navy, the Air Force, the Marine Corps, and the Coast Guard. Their job is to defend and protect the United States at home and abroad.

To join the military, you must meet certain requirements. You must be at least 18 years old (or 17 with your parents' permission) and be a citizen of the United States. Although there are some exceptions, you have to have been born in the United States or, if born in another country, have become a legal citizen later. The military can refuse to let you join if you owe a lot of money in the form of bank loans, credit cards, and so on. You cannot join if you are a single parent. You are also likely to be rejected if you have a criminal history or a problem with drugs or alcohol.

There are height requirements you must meet, too. Generally, you must be at least 60 inches (152 centimeters) tall but less than 80 inches (203 cm). Weight is not as much of a concern, as the military will make sure you eventually work off any excess you may have.

If you meet these basic requirements, the military will then put you through several tests. Some concern your overall health. Others are designed to examine your personality. For example, the military wants to know if you are the type of person who works well as part of a team. It wants to be sure you are good at following orders. The military also tries to determine your natural talents. People who are naturally good at math, for example, might become **engineers**. Those who are quick and athletic might make good combat soldiers. People who have an understanding of machines and good leadership skills might become helicopter crew chiefs.

Crew chiefs need strong mechanical skills.

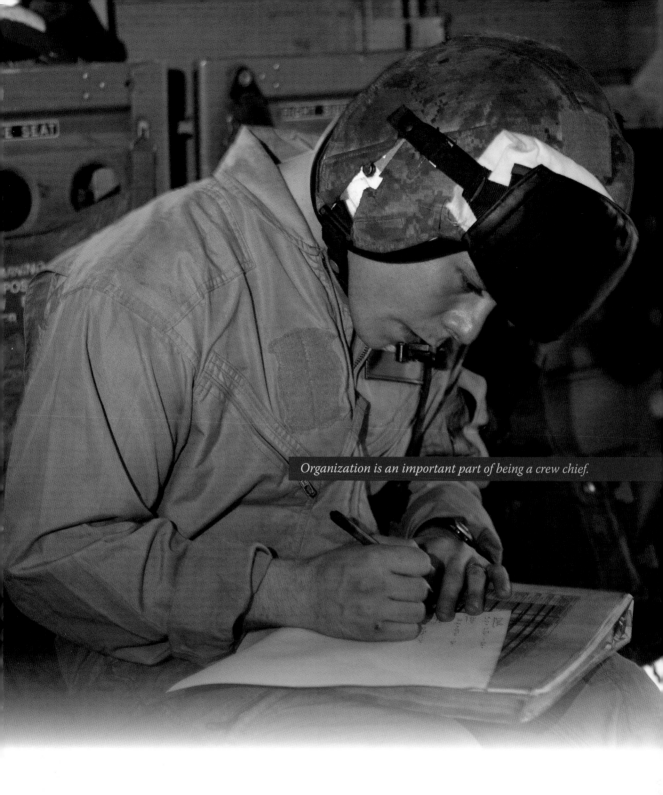

Organization is an important part of being a crew chief.

All crew chiefs need normal **color perception**. Much of the equipment a crew chief uses has colored lights and other color-coded features, so proper eyesight is very important. It does not make a difference whether you're male or female. A crew chief can be either. As far as **rank** is concerned, a crew chief can be any enlisted person, from a private to a sergeant. An officer, someone who holds a leadership position in the military, would be considered too high in rank for the position.

LEARNING & INNOVATION SKILLS

There are times when military training will seem more like torture than anything else. Basic training is the physical and mental preparation you'll receive for several weeks immediately after you've joined the military. It's designed not only to get you ready for your military career but also to find out if you've got the right stuff to succeed in the armed forces. Some people drop out before basic training is finished. Many quit within the first few days. Those who tough it out, however, usually enjoy rewarding careers in the years that follow.

Crew chiefs need to know how to operate weapons in case they have to take part in combat.

If the military determines that you are a potential crew chief, you will begin training. You will learn how to operate equipment while in a moving military aircraft, which can provide a very bumpy and unsettling ride. You will be taught how to manage people and how to be organized. You will learn helicopter basics and then details about the type of helicopter to which you'll be assigned.

Because a crew chief has to be familiar with the mechanical workings of a helicopter, many believe the chief first needs hands-on experience as an actual mechanic. This is not necessarily true, but experience does help. The military will be more likely to consider you for a crew chief's position if you've done this kind of work before. In fact, some helicopter

Sometimes crew chiefs have to perform repairs during a flight.

mechanics have been around helicopters for so long that they can tell one type from another simply by the sound of the blades and the engine. If you don't have mechanical experience, you'll still be required to achieve a high score on a mechanical-maintenance test.

A crew chief must be able to handle a variety of difficult situations, including some that have nothing to do with taking care of a helicopter. For example, you will need to develop a certain level of swimming expertise in case your helicopter goes down in the water. You must know survival basics in the event that the helicopter goes down in the wild. If you crash and members of the crew are injured, you will be expected to perform emergency medical procedures. If enemy forces capture you, you will have to know how to resist **interrogation**.

A helicopter crew chief usually has to qualify for high **security clearance**. Some of the advanced electronics used in modern military copters is cutting-edge technology and therefore top secret. The military needs to know it can trust you completely. They will do a complete and thorough check on your background, talking to people who know you and browsing through every available record. Secret information that gets leaked to an enemy can mean lost battles—and lost lives.

CHAPTER THREE
A DAY ON THE JOB

Being a helicopter crew chief can be both exciting and interesting. Over the course of his or her career,

Apache helicopters are used to complete dangerous combat missions.

a crew chief may work on several different types of helicopters. One of the most common is the Blackhawk, which is often used for attack purposes. Blackhawks are also put to work in medical evacuations, troop and cargo transport, command and control missions, and **reconnaissance** missions. Another common military helicopter is the Apache, a fearful fighting machine that carries night-vision systems, automatic cannons, and laser-guided missiles.

 LIFE & CAREER SKILLS

One of the greatest life skills taught by the military is the habit of checking and rechecking your work. Mistakes can be very costly, particularly when lives are on the line. Every detail counts, and you'll be expected to learn how to do things correctly. This will require you to not only master your skills but also review your work over and over. This may sound boring and difficult, but you'll take great pride in knowing that whatever work you've done, you've done right.

Before any helicopter gets off the ground, the crew chief is responsible for performing a **preflight check**. Every piece of equipment on the craft is closely examined. Electronics are tested, fluid levels are measured, and windows are cleaned. The crew chief has a list to check, and the chief and the team go over it one item at a time. When they are finished, it is not unusual for them to go through the list again . . . and maybe even a third time. If a crew chief discovers any serious problems, the helicopter has to stay grounded. The pilot is in charge of the

Crew chiefs always inspect helicopters before takeoff.

craft when it is in the air, but the crew chief is the boss the rest of the time.

When the bird is ready to fly, the crew chief either hops aboard and takes part in the mission or remains on the ground. A crew chief who remains on the ground will often act as the pilot's "eyes and ears" during takeoff. Because of the design of some helicopters, a pilot may have trouble seeing everything that's around. In that case, the crew chief has to guide the pilot. This can be dangerous for the crew chief, because he or she has to stand fairly close to a very powerful machine.

Once the helicopter lifts off, the crew chief and the rest of the team salute the pilot and any others who are on board. This is not only standard procedure in the military but also a sign of respect to the flight crew who may be heading into danger.

Other times, a crew chief takes part in a flying mission. In these instances, the crew chief is most likely positioned somewhere toward the back of the helicopter. The front is where the pilot, copilot, and other flight crew sit. The crew chief's duty is the same in the air as it is on the ground: to make sure the bird operates properly. He or she monitors all equipment and makes adjustments when necessary. If there are malfunctions or other emergencies, the crew chief has to know exactly how to handle them.

The crew chief also has to keep the pilot aware of the copter's limitations. Knowing what it can and can't do saves lives. This is one of the crew chief's most important jobs, as the pilot has to have realistic expectations of the craft that is being flown. A crew chief must be prepared to take on other duties during tense moments, such as firing weapons or tending to medical emergencies.

At the end of a mission, the crew chief and team have to perform their point-by-point check of the helicopter again. This is called the **postflight check**. Sometimes a helicopter will be required to fly more than once in the same day—sometimes within a matter of hours. During wartime, a helicopter might come back with damage from enemy fire. The crew chief needs to evaluate the damage and get the bird back into operating condition as soon as possible.

Even under normal circumstances, parts have to be replaced, equipment tests run, and fresh fuel and other fluids added. If a crew chief doesn't have enough time to go through every item on the checklist, he or she has to know which items are the most important. For every hour that a helicopter spends in the air, about five hours are spent maintaining it!

When the crew chief is finished working on the helicopter for the day, he or she has to fill out paperwork detailing that day's events. Even if the bird never took off and only the most basic maintenance was performed, a log of everything must be made. Only after this final task is completed can a crew chief get some rest. By that time, the helicopter's other crew has taken over, enabling the military to keep every bird ready to fly 24 hours a day, seven days a week!

Helicopters often need to be washed after they return from missions.

CHAPTER FOUR
LOOKING TOWARD THE FUTURE

I t's difficult to predict how many helicopter crew chief positions will be available in the future. The military's demand

Helicopter crew chiefs, like other military workers, are in higher demand during times of war.

for any position is based on its needs at the time. During times of war, those demands grow. During times of peace, they shrink. Sometimes the military's needs are so small that people who want to join have to put their names on a waiting list.

21ST CENTURY CONTENT

In 2010, the military's Sikorsky X2 helicopter broke a speed record by traveling at just under 300 miles (483 kilometers) per hour. It accomplished this feat with the aid of digital flight controls, a "pusher propeller" at the back, and several other high-tech innovations. As these types of developments occur, the military will discard older helicopters in favor of new-and-improved models. Helicopter crew chiefs who take time to improve their skills in order to keep up with these developments will give themselves an edge over others in their position.

Joining the military has many benefits, regardless of whether you become a helicopter crew chief or something entirely different. You will receive free training in a specific field, and you might even qualify for a free college education.

The military will provide you with clothing, meals, and a place to live. Your health benefits will also be covered. If you stay in the military long enough, you'll even receive retirement benefits. And, depending on where your assignments are located, you may very well get the chance to travel around the world.

In addition to these benefits, the military will pay you a salary. A person's military earnings are based on his or her

Helicopter crew chiefs often travel to faraway nations.

Some of the mechanical skills that crew chiefs develop can also be used on other machines.

rank and on the amount of time served. For example, a private who recently enlisted makes very little compared to a general who has been in the service for his or her entire adult life. On average, a helicopter crew chief makes between $35,000 and $45,000 per year. The salary might be adjusted based on factors such as how badly the military needs crew chiefs, whether the nation is at war, and so on.

The skills you learn during a military career will be useful when you leave the armed forces. A former helicopter crew chief, for example, is qualified for a position working for an airline or designing new aircraft. Many private businesses hire people with military experience. They know that a former soldier has not only professional skills but also valuable personal traits, such as discipline and an appreciation for the importance of hard work.

The technology used in military helicopters is constantly evolving and improving. This is absolutely necessary if our armed forces are to be the best in the world. As a result, the military is always in need of good people. A helicopter crew chief plays an important role, bravely helping to ensure the safety of the nation.

Do you have what it takes to become a helicopter crew chief?

GLOSSARY

blades (BLAYDZ) the flat, paddle-shaped arms of a helicopter's propeller

color perception (KUHL-ur pur-SEP-shuhn) the ability to see colors

engineers (en-juh-NEERZ) people who design and build machines or large structures

hover (HUHV-ur) to remain in one place in the air

interrogation (in-ter-uh-GAY-shuhn) the questioning of someone in an attempt to gain information

postflight check (POST-flite CHEK) an inspection of a helicopter after it returns from a flight

preflight check (PREE-flite CHEK) an inspection of a helicopter before it takes off for a flight

rank (RANGK) an official job level or position

reconnaissance (ri-KON-uh-zuhnts) a survey of an area to gather information

security clearance (si-KYOOR-uh-tee KLIR-unts) the status of a person in regard to how much access to secret information they are allowed

tarmac (TAR-mac) the area of an airfield where aircraft take off and land

FOR MORE INFORMATION

BOOKS

Abramovitz, Melissa. *Military Helicopters*. Mankato, MN: Capstone Press, 2012.

Bodden, Valerie. *Helicopters*. Mankato, MN: Creative Education, 2012.

Gonzalez, Lissette. *The U.S. Military: Defending the Nation*. New York: PowerKids Press, 2008.

Peppas, Lynn. *Military Helicopters: Flying into Battle*. New York: Crabtree Publishing, 2011.

WEB SITES

Marine Corps Crew Chiefs
http://usmilitary.about.com/od/marines/a/crewchiefs.htm
Get an inside look at the job of a U.S. Marine helicopter crew chief, with quotes from people who perform that job.

Military Careers
www.militarycareersinfo.com
Find out more about different jobs in the military, job requirements, branches of the armed forces, and schooling.

Today's Military
www.todaysmilitary.com
Check out this site for advice about choosing a military career and for current information on recent trends and developments in all branches of the armed forces.

INDEX

ABOUT THE AUTHOR

Wil Mara is the award-winning author of more than 120 books, many of which are educational titles for young readers. Information about his work can be found at www.wilmara.com.